# Jack
## BRINGS THE RINGS

### By Mindy Weiss
### Illustrated by Siski Kalla

3 BOYS

Illustrations by Siski Kalla

Published by 3 Boys, Los Angeles

Edited and designed by Girl Friday Productions
www.girlfridayproductions.com

Design: Paul Barrett

ISBN (hardcover): 978-1-7361906-1-6

To Jack and all that follow in your family.
Your smile and joy have inspired me to write a book
about a little boy's journey down the aisle.
Your grammy and I
dream about moments like these. Enjoy!


Auntie Min Min

In Jack's bright blue house there was lots going on.
His parents were cooking and singing a song!

Jack loved their hot pancakes. His tummy agreed!
So, he jumped out of bed, his short feet full of speed.

Jack stopped in his tracks with balloons left and right,
But pushed through and found a breakfast delight!

There were colorful plates and some glasses stacked high.
He tilted his head. "A . . . ah . . . party, but why?"

"They're coming!" said Mom. "So, get dressed right away!
It's a shower for Ali and Jesse's special day!"

Jack huffed and he puffed as he marched down the hall.
"A shower? No way! I'd rather play ball!"

With baseball and mitt, Jack got ready to play,
But Ali and Jesse had something to say.

"We need a ring bearer and want you to hold
The rings for our wedding. They're diamond and gold!"

"Ring bearer? What's that? Would I dress like a bear?
With bells on the paws? Like a mascot with flair?"

Then Ali and Jesse both gave him a smile.
"No costumes, just walking our rings down the aisle."
Jack couldn't say, "Yes!" He was way too afraid.
"I'll think about it," was the promise he made.

Once Ali and Jesse were gone from the house,
Jack sought out his mother and clung to her blouse.

"So, Mom, why do Ali and Jesse want me?"
"We're bestest of friends, and it's custom, you see."

"Like baseball you're placed in the spot you fit best.
The bridal team needs you, so fill their request.

We'll practice and help you to act the right way.
We want you prepared for this wonderful day!"

"You'll wear a tuxedo or some kind of suit.
You'll take a few photos, so smile . . . big and cute!"

"You'll carry their rings on a pillow with lace.
It's not a long walk, not even one base.

The rings are all snuggled and tied really tight.
So, don't be afraid, it'll all turn out right."

"When wedding day comes, we will watch and feel proud.
We'll give you a cheer, but we can't be too loud."

Jack fiddled his fingers, then made up his mind.
"Okay, I will do it." He couldn't decline.

The wedding day came and went off with no hitch,
And Jack enjoyed eating the cake that was rich.

He danced to the music and joined in the laughter,
As Ali and Jesse began their great EVER AFTER!

Inside this frame,
your picture you'll lay,
To remind you of that
special wedding day!

CPSIA information can be obtained
at www.ICGtesting.com
Printed in the USA
BVHW021406010721
610976BV00006B/847